LOOKING IN
FROM
OUTSIDE

POETRY & PROSE

DONNA LAWRENCE

Crescent Hill Press

Published by Crescent Hill Press, LLC
Visit the author's website at: donnamarielawrence.com.
Copyright © 2024 by Donna Lawrence

Cover Art: Photo of eucalyptus branch courtesy of Annie Spratt @unsplash.com. Color by Donna Lawrence.
ISBN # 979-8-9872168-3-5 (paperback)
ISBN# 979-8-9872168-4-2 (eBook)

Disclaimer:
This book is a work of fiction. Names, characters, places, and incidents are the product of the author's imagination or used fictitiously. Certain events, characters, and dialogue were created to lend authenticity to this work. Any resemblance or similarities to actual events or persons, living or dead, are entirely coincidental.

All adjectives referencing ethnic or racial groups are capitalized to delineate race from the color of an object. Therefore, Black and White are capitalized when denoting race. They are not meant to be offensive to today's reader(s).

Also by

DONNA LAWRENCE

Miss Virginia and the Sweet Sisters: A Novel

COMING SOON:

Pen Pals: A Novella and Other Stories

Light from an Unburned Candle: A Novel

DEDICATION

To My Mother,

Nora Frances Harris

and

To All Who Have Loved

And Lost. To Those Who Have Triumphed And

Shown Courage When Faced With Life's Challenges—

Here's To You.

TABLE OF CONTENTS

PREFACE

Through what lens should we view life? The one that
seldom looks back—except to find joy.

Before novels of fiction, there was poetry–at least for me.
It is said that reading a poem should evoke a feeling that
brings about emotions you never knew you had. The
author's random thoughts are solidified into a cohesive
whole that stirs the imagination through rhythm, rhyme,
and image. The words expressed are personal to the
author but subjective to the reader.

Some of these pieces were written long ago but still
hold merit today. A few are firsthand experiences; others
are pure imagination, told with an authenticity that is
sometimes raw with emotion. This is *not* my story but
reflections on my feelings and perspectives about life.

I hope this endeavor prompts the reader to think
and discern what came only from my imaginative vision
written when reflection was needed, perspective was
warranted, and relating to each other seemed necessary.

So, welcome to a collective mix of poetry and prose
on several themes, chronicling one woman's journey
from a young age to adulthood as she accepts her
strength and purpose through courage and perseverance
amid tragedy and self-discovery.

In these written words, may the reader find
inspiration and the idea of a promising tomorrow.

~The Author

✸ Family ✸

And if I sing,

you are my

voice.

The Choice

IT WAS BLUE. A very light blue with white floaty things swirling around like clouds. I knew nothing of entities, God, or angels, but I did know I was comforted. I also remember thinking I didn't want to feel pain. Particularly like I had felt before. In my other life, perhaps? But it was important enough to ask, even though it was a distant memory. The Voice knew all too well what I had suffered. After my question, He answered vaguely, giving me a choice (free will). I remember sighing as my spirit weighed the decision I had chosen. But I was resigned to my fate, saying this was necessary because "I belonged there."

THE VOICE: Do you know where you want to go?

    Me: Yes. There.

THE VOICE: Why there?

    Me: Because they need me.

THE VOICE: If you are sure.

    Me: Yes. …Will there be pain?

THE VOICE: Not like before, though it will be hard.

    Me: No pain?

THE VOICE: There will be some pain, but different.

    Me: (Pause as I consider this answer.)

THE VOICE: You must choose now.

    Me: That's where I belong.

THE VOICE: Are you ready?

    Me: Yes.

3

I've often wondered if this happened, but then I catch myself and chase away that doubt. Of course, it did. When I look at babies, I'm struck by this memory and wonder if they've had this experience or something like it. And if so, will they remember?

My entire life has been spent wondering how I knew I was needed by my chosen family.

Until I find and understand that answer, I know my life on Earth is not yet done.

A Mother's Voice

It's the voice you hear upon conception.
It's the voice like that of doves.
It's the tender voice of acceptance.
It's the unfettered voice of love.

It's the voice that catches you up short,
When naughtiness is near.
It's the voice that you respect always,
When uncertainty appears.

It's the voice that shows concern and fear,
When everything seems all but lost.
It's the voice that echoes in your ears,
When encouragement is sought.

It's the voice you've known all your life.
It's the voice of laughter at its best.
It's the voice of song and sweet caress.
A voice that's better than the rest.

This voice is nectar for your soul,
        It's the one you have come to trust...
                From Mom.

A Child Is Born

You came in like a whisper.
    As quiet as a mouse.
Tiptoeing across my heartstrings,
    My love, no one could doubt.

It was easy and so right
    To love you right away.
You made me laugh a time or two,
    Your smile on full display.

On that day, you stole my heart,
    When I kissed your little head.
And since that day, I never knew,
    The joy you'd bring instead.

The tears I shed before you came
    Are distant memories now.
The long wait for your arrival,
    Got me through somehow.

The years have flown, and I can't forget
    The moments of that day.
You are my treasure, my hope, and love,
    Long after I've passed away.

For My Mom

What were you like as a girl?

Did you tell silly jokes?
    Did you laugh out loud?
Did you have big dreams,
    Gazing up at the clouds?

Did you walk barefoot,
    In grass of dew?
Did you like sunshine,
    Or soft rain too?

Did you have lots of friends,
    Or wonderful grades?
Were you popular or shy,
    Or unafraid?

Did boys hide from you?
    Or you from them?
Did you keep many secrets?
    Or tell on a whim?

Did you run with abandon,
    Or just skip along?
Did you dream of Prince Charming,
    Or sing crazy songs?

Were you often sad and lonely,
    Wishing for better days?
Did you question life's purpose?
    Have you ever lost your way?

If you ponder life's mysteries
    Of where that girl has gone,
You needn't look very far.
    For she lives inside me,
                Ever safe and strong.

Grandma Says

People say I'm not Black,
But yes, ma'am, I am.
All parts of me,
Yellow and tan.

People say a lot of things.
But my papa and mama
Take no never mind
Those who want to shame.

They are my own,
And proud I be
To call them
For their name.

All parts of me
And yes, I claim
The mixture
That they bring.

The air I breathe
Is no lesser than
Those who want
To take a stand.

I say to hell with them!
For who I am, ain't
No business for today.
It's my taint, my fate to carry
    …Anyway!

The Enigma

Growing up, it was always, what are you?
Always wanting to know
Where I came from.
What language did I speak?

Growing up, it was always, who are your parents?
Always wanting to know
Which one was white.
What island were they from?

Growing up, it was always, can I feel your hair?
Always wanting to know
Why the color was so blue black.
Was it dyed or straightened?

Growing up, it was always about my appearance.
Always wanting to know—why,
My nails were so pink, the tips so white.
Is that a French manicure?

Tiresome really.
What difference does it make?
Telling the truth makes no sense to most.
Always questions, so let me boast.

Mô Djè!

My name is my name.
Creole is my ethnicity, and Black is my race.
I am a proud woman of color,
From the house of Dáviès,
Pass the hot sauce, please…

That should be enough.

Inner Glow

Children light the world with smiles and drown it
with tears.

Cherish, protect, and nurture the child in your life,
and remember the one from your youth…

So that you never forget how to live.

Hands and Arms

Hands and Arms.
Those words should be easy to say,
But they aren't.
At six years old, I should be able to,
      But I can't.

Hands and Arms reach out and slap.
Hands and Arms hurt me.
Hands and Arms push and throw.
Hands and Arms are mean.

Hands and Arms
Enfold to keep us safe from harm,
But they don't.
I'm supposed to trust them,
      But I can't.

Hands and Arms swing wildly.
Hands and Arms don't miss.
Hands and Arms scare me.

      I don't like Hands and Arms.

❧ Home ❧

Tricycles, bicycles,
dances
and swings…

Memories
are
made of these
things.

School Rules

Trying to fit in isn't easy.
Am I the only one they watch?
But I don't care if they stare.
      It's not my problem.

I'm different, I know.
Not so much it shows.
I want to be left alone,
If only for more than a minute.

Why is my voice laughed about?
Why is my look so mocking?
Why are my actions talked about?
Why are my thoughts so shocking?

They shouldn't be, for you see,
I'm not the one with questions.
Figuring it out, there's no need to shout.
      I'm more than your average vermin.

Trying to fit in isn't easy.
Am I the only one they watch?
But I don't care if they stare.
      It's not my problem.

I'm different, I know.
Not so much it shows.
I want to be left alone,
If only for more than a minute,
      In these halls of learning.

Laughter

I like the sound of my laughter,
When it comes from underneath.
I like it when I hoot out loud,
Unfettered, messy, and deep.

I like to hear it crawling out.
I like the staccato hitches and beats.
I like to hear it hiccup uncontrolled,
Blurted out like the pounding of meat.

I like to slap my thigh in a guffaw.
I like the pleasant feeling it gives.
I like the tears that are bound to fall,
Tightening my belly to nibs.

I like the snort, the giggle, the windedness.
I like the aching for it to cease.
I like the easing up and starting again,
By the memory of the piece.

Yes. Like a child.

I like the sound of laughter,
When it comes from underneath.
I like to hear it hoot out loud,
Unfettered, messy, and deep.

Donna Lawrence

Teenage Waze
(To Live Forever)

Fast cars and evening stars,
And picking petty fights.
Gauging others from afar,
Tough owners of the night.

Full moon shining bright.
Who can quelch our dreams?
Larger than the Dipper's sight
Is fortune and our schemes.

Although well-formed our bodies are,
How surely IN security sets in.
But that won't beat the sweet guitar,
And being owners of our sins.

Fast forward, we dare not dwell,
For promises are our claim.
Today is for the living,
And tomorrow is the same.

Small Packages

Late-night talks in the open air.
A front porch invites us to stare,
Into the sky of the quiet night.
We are awed by this universal sight.

Katydid sounds and chigger bites.
Who's to tell us what was right?
Neighbors watched and scared us so,
For we were young with much to know.

The church bells rang out a tune,
A harbinger of lazy afternoons.
Shops on corners and giddy delight
Of ice cream, soda pops, and candy fights.

We grew up there long ago,
Now wistfully pulled into the throes
Of a small town with timeless dots...
And memories of lonely
                    forget-me-nots.

Sorority Sisters

Strutting their stuff to a sound all their own,
The loudly spoken Greeks of Eta Rho.
Pink and Green are the colors of the day.
Proud is the Chapter on display.

Distinguished women they represent,
From First Ladies to Second Presidents.
We applaud them for their accomplishments,
For therein lies no impediments.

The sisterhood of which I joined,
A dedication to causes they have coined,
From healthcare to politics, they have toiled,
Idleness they'll not seek to embroil.

Together, they stand, and rightly adored,
These women of Greek will not be scorned.
Never-stopping strides that endlessly flow,
Because there are many miles to go.

...We are Sisters to the end.

Blue Persuasion

What will I find in Colorado,
With the sky as blue as the sea?
Clouds so close you can touch them.
Is this really happening to me?

The air is crisp and good to breathe,
The land spread far and wide.
How surreal this moment feels.
I suppress a chuckle inside.

The churning wheels under me,
Don't diminish this thunderous ride.
As the city comes into view,
It recharges my sense of pride.

Oh, what a sight to see,
This rugged mountain shore.
The peaks stretch north and south,
And I am forever torn.

My homeland is now far away,
As I'm tempted so to stay.
Although green I long to be,
This land holds onto me,
        Reawakened on this day.

My Kentucky Mind

The autumn winds are blowing,
Across my troubled mind.
I've not forgot the sleepy town,
In my Kentucky mind.

Its ups and downs, and all arounds,
The verdant bluegrass molds me.
My childhood days won't pass away,
From my Kentucky mind.

Hold me down.
Wrap me up, console me.
Hold me close.
Let your arms enfold me.

Though streets are bare,
I'm everywhere.
I can't forget the glory.
I've not forgot the sleepy town,
In my Kentucky mind.

Same ups and downs, and all arounds,
These snowy hills can't hold me.
My childhood days won't pass away,
From my Kentucky mind.

I've not forgot the sleepy town,
In my Kentucky mind.

Sunday Dinner at Grandma's

I REMEMBER SUNDAYS. That day before Monday. That quiet day when the church bells rang more loudly, it seemed, than on any other day. After church service, we gathered briefly to greet other members and comment on the sermon, then hurried home to change out of our Sunday clothes to visit Grandma's.

Grandma was either at home or had left church service early to prepare for guests. Us. We were expected. She was excited to have us there. She planned the meal a week before, thinking of everything from soup to nuts. She hurried around her kitchen, checking on gravies, side dishes, desserts, and the main course—meats like roast chicken, baked turkey, pork, lamb chops, roast beef, or glazed ham, for the choosing—no casual fare like tuna casseroles, beef stews, or fried chicken. No, indeed, this was Sunday, and dinner was about to be served.

The door was unlocked, and each family member rushed in to greet Grandma, working hard in the kitchen as if it was no effort at all. Dinner was more than eating. Dinner at Grandma's on Sunday afternoon was a social affair—informal at best, with lots of laughter, jokes, and gossip. I remember the smell of green beans with ham hocks and onions, a roasted chicken in the oven generously basted with butter and pan drippings with more vegetables on the stove, and macaroni & cheese made from scratch, not out of the box. Potatoes were boiled, peeled, mashed, then salted, with butter added for good measure. The dining table, dressed in its finest tablecloth and gleaming silverware, was used only for this occasion. It seemed to smile in thanks for being remembered for use on that day. Then, all was ready. The meal was about to commence.

There were no smartphones, iPads, tablets, or television to distract us. Our focus was on the deliciousness of the food and conversation. We never thought much about the time and effort that went into preparing a meal like that, only the thought of the next day and the drudge of the work week ahead. I don't think we thought about Grandpa, who seemed to take for granted that this Sunday meal would be just so. He enjoyed the day, just like the rest of us, and congratulated Grandma on her efforts while she blushed, saying, "Oh, it was nothing."

We talked to each other, we asked after each other, we were concerned about our futures, and who was moving ahead in either improved school grades or business promotions. We were encouraged to seek our own paths in life and not play "follow the leader" lest we be led off a cliff. We were reminded of family values and teased about our latest boyfriends or girlfriends. We cared about each other, and it showed. The younger kids couldn't wait to finish and play outside, and at the end of the meal, we gathered the dishes to clean while Grandma rested, and Grandpa snored in his *'easy'* chair. We were a clan, a family gathered for one evening of togetherness that bound us forever at the closing of the day. This was the gift of Sunday dinners.

Not only did Grandma prepare a great meal, but she also prepared us to face the days ahead.

We are scattered now, separated by distance, and interactions through conversation are lost. Most of us no longer gather to give silent thanks for what we have in 'family' while sitting at a well-dressed dining table for dinner. We hurriedly eat in the kitchen and reach for our devices for conversation. Even in lockdown, we are separated by technological advances in electronics, which move our focus from ourselves and those we love to the beckoning call of television or smartphones. We care more about what others think of us than those who know us best— our families. We are pulled along to follow and not lead. Grandma didn't push or pull during those Sunday dinners. She wanted us to follow her lead by setting an example, which I fear is lost. An example that says love and caring are tangible and invisible simultaneously. We feel it when surrounded by those sitting with us and talking to show they genuinely care. Are the vestiges of long-ago values forever lost? I hope not. Do we appreciate who we are and what family means? I hope so.

Whatever happened to Sunday dinners at Grandma's? I repeat this question as I look at the dried wishbone taken from a Turkey breast during the last Thanksgiving dinner at Grandma's. It is aged, fragile, and brushed in polyurethane for a long life. And I remember. I remember the days of sunshine and long conversations. I remember the joy on faces that look like mine. I remember the sincere caring and long embrace of good wishes for a better tomorrow.

I remember Grandma in her apron, in her kitchen, smiling at me and welcoming all of us home.

Love

God,

I love being

Female!

The Hat

"Hey, you in the hat," he says as I turn to see him gaze
at me, saying nothing more.
Coming closer, he then says, "You're beautiful."

Well, I don't know if that's all true.
Is it the hat that has him fooled?
Embarrassed,
I look down at the floor.
It's just a hat and nothing more.
Black as night and wide of brim,
The hat has drawn me to him.

And I like that.

The Logic of Nothing

We say hello in the strangest of ways,
Living through the remainder of most days.
Nothing much is made of small passings by.
      Nothing much ever,
          No wondering why.

Before I saw you,
Before you said hello,
Before our eyes met,
Before all was right with the world,
All was nothing.

Before your common sense,
Before your kindness,
Before our common tongues,
Before the knowing,
All was nothing.

Nothing is no more,
If nothing ever was.
Everything is,
Everything is right,
Everything is now.

Everything starts with a word.
Hello is so common.
Hello is something.
     Your hello was something,
        Very everything indeed.

Follow Me

Come follow me and be my love.
Let me guide you to places beyond time.
Hold my hand and take my lead through misty clouds
Of light.
Travel through to my vision and be comforted there,
Unafraid and safe.

For my path is sure and full of purpose.
It holds certainty and promises of never-ending
devotion,
Windswept oasis of joy and peace,
Knowing and understanding all that is and is to be.

Take my hand and follow me.
Travel through this life of time eternal and full.
To oceans of infinite passage and lands of
Endless mystery.
Settle on me all your worries and fears.
Let me shoulder your burdens for a time and teach
How easily they can be tossed.

Let us ride the tide of journeys not yet taken,
And beat out the wonders we have seen but not yet
known.
Walk toward the fires and desolation of the soul,
Only to be found renewed and awakened.
For I see and, what's more, I believe.

Oh yes, this is best!
Oh yes, this is worthy,
You will see.
Close your eyes and be with me.
Travel with your hand in mine.

Travel with my heart in your hand.

29

You

I like the way you move,
The way you walk,
The way you talk,
The ethnic way you express
Yourself,
        The full of you,
                The all of you.

I like the way you smell,
The way you smile,
The way you laugh,
The way you while away the hour
Thinking,
        The sex of you,
                The essence of you.

The pure joy of knowing you,
The excitement of studying you,
The quiet assessment of the wonder of you.
Recognizing the sameness and like mind.
The gentle brush of your lips on my hair,
The way you hold me close,
The way we melt together,
The touch of your body against mine,
The caress, the lingering there,
        And there,
                And there,

                Yes!
I enjoy it all,
        I consume it all,
                And am full…

                Satisfied.

Losing Myself

This passion has been dead for a long time.
This desire has been lost to me for decades.
This burning hunger is stronger than I remember.
This forbidden fruit is so very tempting.

This is much too much for me.
This timeless effort is striking the right chord.
This touching and feeling is my soul's release.
This roaming and finding is my lost control.

This pressure of flesh against mine is exquisite.
This glorious feeling is 'yes' and 'yes' again.
This soft lip is seeking knowledge from me.
This unholy touch is given to me as a gift and

   I…Want…More.

This more is his gaze on me.
This more is his voice against my neck.
This more is his reaching for me.
This more is his hot, burning touch.

This more is my arching against him.
This more is my cry as I reach and reach.
This more is his cry of my name.
This more is my long, suppressed release.

This more is our fall from grace.
This more is my Genie, let loose from its bottle,
This desire,
   This all that I am…
      for him.

31

Donna Lawrence

A Tranquil Tide

I love you in repose.
Thinking quietly of you.
Wondering how it will feel
To hold you again.

I wait for the moment,
And long for it always.
Never knowing how you might
Feel.

I wait patiently, though painfully,
Of time held in a future
That will become part of our
Distant past.

I pine achingly for your touch,
And the quick, gentle brushes
Of your hand.

I love you in repose.
And I think…

I'll think not long on the
Truly unbearable absence
Of you.

A Lament

Cool and cold is the way he said
    Those words I did not want to hear.
Speaking his mind so deftly
    It numbs.

Can I believe what my ears deny?
Calculating old memories,
    Of just minutes passed.

His darkness is terrifying.
    His desire is deep.
I can't see the places
    I long to reach.

Life's games are hard on me.
Developing strength has been slow to come.
Too sweet, too kind, too giving,
Too hard, too cold, too independent
    For my own good.

God is not good.
God is not kind.
Is life worth living?

      Maybe…
           Hell is too easy to find.

Donna Lawrence

Restless Slumber

Misty clouds of grey darken
The early morning sky,
As I sit and, you sleep soundly.

How is it only I am awake
To feel the stabs of late-night pain?
Am I but the shadow you see,
In your technicolor dreamscape?

Sleepers, as dreamers, awaken often
To hold onto that last elusive
Dance of dreams.
Only to find that reality
Is so often unkind.

Will I dream softly
Of love lost and found?
Of dreams captured and released?

The dance of dreams is very well known.
The reality of which is too hard to reap.
My love is gone.

Will I find sleep?

Angry, who's Angry?

When you told me you wanted to be friends.
When you told me you needed space and time.
When you told me you got cold feet.
When you told me you met another,

I wanted to scream (in disgust).

Remembering when you said you loved me.
Remembering when you said you cared.
Remembering when you said how good
I made you feel.
Remembering the good times.
Remembering the tough times too,
And how good it all was.

I wanted to scream (in longing).

When you told me how *perfect* I was for you.
When you told me I had so many *good* qualities.
When you told me we had so much *in common*.
When you told me there was *no other* for you.
When you *held me* tight,

I wanted to scream (in delight).

I can't believe this has happened.
I feel empty, cold, and old.
I feel numb, cynical, and unwanted.
I can't imagine life without you.
I can't imagine my life alone.

Donna Lawrence

I want to scream (in anger).
I cried and cried and prayed to God.
I chanted and chanted to the stars above.
I talked to family, friends, and strangers too.
I did my level best to forget about you.
I did my damnedest to arrange my life back to before,
All to no avail, and so…
I Scream!

I SCReam!

I SCREAM!

For the heart that has been torn
And ripped from my chest.
For the time spent on empty hope,
And false promises.
For the lonely woman who Just. Can't. Seem.
To get it right.

I scream (in despair).
I scream alone.
I scream in silence.
I scream with gaping mouth,

Emitting no discernible sound.

Caressing a Ghost

The early morning cold is not kind.
The air is not as warm as the feel of you.
I toss the night's slumber and vivid comes to mind that
  You are not here upon my waking.

I lie in space between these hollow sheets,
Trying to hold on to deep slumber wishes.
Keeping dreams real is a daunting feat because
  You are not here upon my waking.

My body aches for long, sweet touches
Of natural warmth and heat between my legs.
The soreness along my tense shoulders speaks that
  You are not here upon my waking.

I drag my body up and out of this cocoon of sorrow.
Face the morning mirror and see me standing there,
Far from safe and still heartsore.
My anguished cries resonate from the four walls that
  You are not here upon my waking.

Oh, sleepless night!
Long hours of discomfort
Where is my soul's stillness?
Where does comfort lie?

I get on with my day and while away the hours.
Dinner is tasteless, and I'm very tired.
I dread the night's loneliness,
But try as I might,
Sleep eludes me again because,

  You won't be here upon my waking.

    You won't be here upon my waking.

37

Ring of Change

Here we are,
Looking at this ring on my finger,
And the facets light the air.
How they dance so out there,
       On this finger.

Here we are,
Talking about destruction,
And the message of despair.
How the tears flow down there,
       On this finger.

Here we are,
Talking about devotion,
And the smile in your stare
Is the remnant of what's there,
       On this finger.

Here we are,
Wrapped in so much sorrow,
And the laughter we once shared,
Is an echo heard out there,
       On this finger.

       My empty finger.

One Step Too Far

I stepped off the edge of a cliff,
This time, I stepped too far.
It came as a surprise, naturally,
      For I didn't expect the fall.

I never expected to spill so badly,
All my soulful goods.
I never expected to feel so sadly,
      All my heart endured.

I've come close to this edge before,
So very close the tilting.
I always thought it would catch me,
      The surprise before the wilting.

Now it has, and it's too late.
The free fall of
        wasted
            sands
                of time.
How slowly the decent.
How fast the ground rises.
How soundless the cry for help,

        Then nothing...

I stepped too close to the edge today,
And came out the other side,
Different than what I used to be.
        Anew.

I stepped too close to the edge today.

        I didn't expect the fall....

∾ Losing ∾

They say
it's pretty when it's
played right…

But hell
if you miss that
note.

Donna Lawrence

All That Beckons

I know those city lights,
Are not for me.
They don't seem great.
      So let them be.

I know those city lights,
Leave a bad taste.
Through the many years,
      Of urban waste.

Those shining beacons
That beckon…
      Come.
Those shining beacons
      Tell me I'm the one.

I know those city lights,
Can be mean.
So shiny, pretty, lovely,
      They fit the scene.

I know those city lights,
Ain't complete.
That's why they want me,
      Now, ain't that sweet?

Those shining beacons
That beckon…
      Come.
In those shining beacons
      I succumb.

The Lowest Point

This is not a perfect place to be.
This is not a perfect place to dwell.
This is not a perfect pipe to smoke,
   While you're trying hard to cope.

I can't move.
I can't stand.
I can't fight,
Man to man.

If I could recite
The Lord's Prayer,
   Or the 23rd Psalm.
Hard to decide,
But I swear…
   It gets me by.

I can't swear.
I don't dare.
My throat bleeds.
When it tears.

I won't tell.
If I do,
I'll lose him,
This is true.
But I swear…
   It gets me by.

This is not the perfect place to breathe.
I'm tired of being on my knees.
This is not the perfect place to hope,
   When you're trying not to choke.

43

Donna Lawrence

Make It Stop

I go on crying for hours at a time.
Nothing works, nothing hurts.
Nothing moves inside.
Can't do nothing but hope,
This will be all right.

How can I love you,
When you beat me
How can I want you,
When you beat me

It's agony wondering what to do.
I can't think; I can't move,
And I blame myself.
Can't do nothing but want,
To be somewhere else.

How many times did I hurt you?
When did I ever push you…
HARD?
How many times did I curse you?
When will these bruises…
FADE?

I only know what I must do.
Knowing full well
I'll never escape you.
All I know is that I'm worth,
More than this.

How can I love you,
When you beat me
How can I trust you,
When you…
beat me

44

Too Much Fun

I was out…
At the club…
Having fun…
Lots of fun.
Just the girls
And me.

I felt hazy.
It was crazy.
I said goodbye.
He asked, "Can I walk you to your car?"

He had a knife.
Wish I could fight.
He was bigger than me.
He was stronger than me.
I said, "Oh My God!"

When I awoke…
I was numb…
There were cuts everywhere.
There was so much blood.
How do I get home?

I had to walk…
I had to crawl…
Got to find my way…
Got to find my
Car.

Donna Lawrence

This is the part
Where I blame myself.
This is the part,
There is no one else.

The dress, the booze,
The walk, the shoes,
The hair, the gloss.
WHO was the boss?

"OH MY GOD!"

That's enough…
Just enough…
He was to blame!
He was the shame!

At the club…
Having fun…
He saw me there…
The swing of my hair…
He said, "Oh My God."

I felt hazy.
It was crazy.
I said goodbye.
He asked, "Can I walk you to your car?"

He had a knife….

Healing

Bright lights engulf me.
    I am alone.
Voices call out but,
        All is silent again.

Awake, I lie in satin cloth.
        Cold is warmth and fire.
Feeling is hard, I can't cope,
        All is silent, but then…

Blue is comforting.
    No longer alone,
I feel love around me.
        All is silent again.

Dreams are nightmares.
    I don't like red.
I stare at nothing.
        All is silent, but then…

                Sun.

Donna Lawrence

Pissed As Hell

I stand here and hear you, but I'm not listening.
I stand here and see you, but I see nothing.
You use words,
You use hate,
You sell yourself short.

Surely you can do better.

How dare you speak this way!
How dare you sound so full of you!
Why do I hear this?
Why do I care that you're angry?

Why indeed.

I curse you; I despise you, I spit on you,
And yet you have the nerve to do this to me
You ignorant piece of shit!
I should slap your face, kick, and scream at you,
But the damage had been done
        Hasn't it?

I say this, and you say that,
And are saying it still!
Well, shout!
        Yell it out loud!
                        Louder!!
                                Louder still!!!
And watch as I walk away.
Words are words, after all.
Silence is the thing that kills.

Silence is the best bitch of all.

Painting Exercises

She painted her nails red today,
Fingers and her toes.
No particular reason other than
To chase away her woes.

She searched for something,
To occupy her time.
Next, she'll reach for a larger bottle
Of that very nice red wine.

He's leaving and going far away,
Packed his bags and his belongings.
He's on his way to that southern place,
Hastening time and not prolonging.

Such annoyance, all of this,
His leaving and relieving.
Why bother with farewells?
It's only himself he's deceiving.

He just might marry in that southern place.
She just might forget.
She's painting and re-arranging,
Not bothering with regret.

For now, she'll paint her future bright,
Until she gets it right.
Not particularly liking nail polish,
      Especially red at night.

The Pretender

Love is a demon.
A viper and deceiver of the heart.
Love is a pretender and liar.
The great master of deception and art.

Once it takes
The sweetness of your soul,
You're forever bound to its embrace.
      Shaken and mistaken, losing control.

Love is father and mother.
The giver of wonderful things.
It promises to never falter.
Hiding the heartbreak it brings.

It tells us
This is what we need,
This is all there is,
      And
           that Hell is no better place,

              …than this.

Dark Consumption

Is this what it's like after many years,
To discover you were never loved.
> Ever!

Is this what it's like at the bottom of the pit,
Gasping for air in the black abyss?
> Is this what it's like?

I never want to be here again.
I never want to be in this state of mind.
Alone, trying to deafen the noise.
Of screeching, searing pain.

Eating myself alive with regret.

> Oh no, not ever again!

This is not what I planned.
Abused, battered, played upon, and pitied.
This is not the way it was supposed to be.

> I've got to get out of this place,

> Now!

Donna Lawrence

Seeking Awareness

Every now and then, someone will look up.
A sound, a cry, or noise will cause them to jump.
Every now and then, someone will look down,
Unaware that anyone is around.

Every now and then, we make a choice,
A feeble attempt to use our voice.
Every now and then, we dance around,
Incapable of making a sound.

Every now and then, we ask why,
Understanding reasons for lost time.
Every now and then, we are surprised,
By what's occurring before our very eyes!

Every now and then, a nut the blind will find.
Every now and then, from sand the head will rise.
Every now and then, we sidestep the venomous snake.
Every now and then, the sleeper finally awakes.

...Every now and then.

Bridges Burned

I thought I saw you yesterday.
You didn't see me,
I've nothing to say.

Why can't I tell you?
Live and learn.
I thought I saw you.
        Bridges Burned.

It's kind of funny,
So they say.
Life doesn't deal you,
Quite a fair shake.

I never thought I'd
Lose like this.
Oh, what I'd give,
For just one kiss.

Did we help it along the way?
Was it you who couldn't stay?
Was it me that hurt you so?
Or did our love refuse to grow?

I thought I saw you yesterday.
You didn't see me,
I've nothing to say.

Why can't I face you?
Lesson learned.
I thought I saw you.
        Bridges Burned.

Friends

Sometimes…

You just gotta
laugh!

It's a smile for the soul.

S

P

O

N'tan

E

Ity!

A Toast

(At a Dinner of Four but No More)

Here's to we two!

Now, if you two like we two...

Then here's to we four.

But if you two don't like we two, like we two like
you two,

Then here's to we two, and no more.

Model Daze

I am no one special.
  Not anyone's wannabe.
I've failed almost every test,
  While starving to be the best.

I am no one special.
  I have flaws like everyone else.
Although the camera loves me,
  My life's an endless mess.

This isn't really me.
  I question every turn.
From inside and out,
  I wrestle with doubt.

Encased in success and glamour,
  Living this 'High Life,' of stammer.
If only they knew the truth,
  These fleeting bastions of youth.

Don't look at me with envy,
  It's a wasted exercise.
In gossamer threads fully made up,
  Think, "How empty is her cup?"

I am no one special.
  You can trust me on this.
My aloof stare doesn't matter,
  Wrapped in fluff and flatter.

I am no one special.
  Thou you might think it true.
I am just another person.
  Longing to be just like you.

We Meet

Pure electricity.
Fire and Ice.
Amazing white teeth.
Slim hips. Nice nose.

I'm drawn to him.
I'm taken in by his transformation.
Where did he come from?
Who is he? I must know.

From the stage, he comes to me.
Embarrassed beyond belief.
How many shades of red are there
in the world?
Attraction. So profound.

What's happening here?

He wants to meet me, take me out
For drinks.
I must say no, but I can't.
He can't like me.
He must never like me. Does he know?
I think not.

Why now in my life?
Yes! Now in my life.
I must know more about him.
Is he interested?
Will he call?

God, I hope so.

Donna Lawrence

Bear Tooth in the Sky

I love this land,
This Montana.
Wide, open spaces and skies.
What a moment this is.

The wind in my hair,
The freedom I feel,
The love from so many
Is infectious.

The welcome of sunshine,
Embraces my soul,
And I move effortlessly.
Freeing the bonds of constriction,

I'm me.

All life should be this easy,
It should be this glorious, too.
I should always feel this happy,
In chasing away the blues.

But sadly, I must depart.
With memories in my heart,
I will always ache for the music,
In the song Montana sings.

Prisms
(Of Us)

What color is your rainbow?
What colors are your stripes?
What colors are the fallen leaves,
In the autumn of your night?

What colors are your trees?
What colors are your blooms?
What color do you see,
In the calm late afternoons?

What color, yes indeed,
Is the color of your door?
The one we pass through,
Today and evermore?

What color is your portal,
That beckons over time?
As it draws you even closer,
It operates the same as mine...

Regardless of the color.

Whirlwinds

You bubble all over the place and worry about
everything.
Concise and neat, you place your life in an orderly
arrangement of things.
I wonder how sad you are not stopping to breathe in
the quiet.
Needing desperately to be:

lovedandmarriedandchildfilledandblessedandorderlyand
neatand,and—

Whew!

You are lovely and full of life.
You've got so much to give.
Your star brightly and shines on us all.
I pity those who don't see it, for they miss the most
beautiful sight of your selflessness and pure,
pure genius of:

organizingarrangingnotstoppingtobreathelistingandnum
bering—and we love you for it.

Don't ever stop being you.

Life Without Friends

Where would we be without friends?
    Those unsung keepers of our secrets and dreams.
Those fierce warriors who protect our virtue,
    Ensuring the worst is not as bad as it seems?

Where would we be without the friends we have?
    Those kindred spirits, much like our own.
Those restless companions who push us toward,
    Being the best person, they've come to know?

The supporters of our wishes,
    The comforters of our fears,
Their timeless visages are always there,
    When we need them near.

Where would we be without friends, you see?
    Those timekeepers of our shared laughter.
Those sages of wisdom and speakers of truth,
    Listeners to wishes for our ever-after's.

Where would we be without them?
    Those friends we cherish most,
Those friends who call out our faults,
    With honest and wonderful boasts!
        Those dependable, loyal, and faithful...
            Friends.

The Wedding

My friend is getting married today.
We are all anxious, nervous, and rushed,
While she remains calm. Outwardly beautiful
and serene. I stand here thinking about the days
we've shared leading up to this
moment.
My friend is getting married today. The heady
excitement that's felt covers all the hectic, scream-at-
you, scream-at-them days before this special day.
Covers all the frustrations and pitfalls that planning
a wedding can bring. Covers all the hurt feelings,
resentment, and pent-up anxiety of why-her-and-not-
me feelings that one or two of us remaining four have
felt.
My friend is getting married today to a remarkable man.
And if she were my own sister, I couldn't be more
pleased with the match. He is kind, wonderful,
thoughtful, reflective, resourceful, and wise. He is a
rock and her very center. My guy is not so, but he is
mine, warts, and all. On this day, he's my knight in
shining armor. The love of my
life.
My friend is getting married today, and my feelings run
very deep. She is my best friend, and I wish her all the
best. I would walk through fire for her. I would take on
all comers and good riddance to the goers. I will stand
with her and support her. I will stand with her and,
in her sense of purpose, glory in the ceremony. I
will stand with them and, like a specter of light,
hold up their truth to the
world.
Yes, I will stand with her and dare anyone to speak ill
Of this union,

Of this
Celebration,

Of this
Her marriage,

Of this
Our friendship.

64

The Riches

Caviar and pate,
    With a side of barbecue wings?
Beer and Wine
    Whites and Reds are only the best of things.

Who are these people,
    Standing around pretending to be better?
Who are these people,
    Side eyes glancing, sniffing the air in a fetter?

Salmon and asparagus,
    Chicken breast and shaved beef, too?
Also, Olives, (my dear)
    Green and Black, for only the best, will do.

Who are these people,
    Wandering around to strike a pose or two?
Who are these people,
    Feigning surprise over an acquaintance's hair do?

Teacakes and cucumber sandwiches,
    A burger or two with pickles you could make.
And cake, (why not)
    White, of course, so there is no mistake.

Pretentiousness of the highest order,
    I dare say I'm impressed.
But I find myself easily amused,
    Laughing at this mess.

As famous poets have often spoke,
    How others may come to see us.
Lest we forget, always,
            Things flaunted just to peeve us.

Green Eyes

It's something that sneaks up on you.
    It catches you unaware.
All at once, it finds you,
    And whispers in your ear.

It's something that steals your worth.
    It causes you to swear.
All at once, you're acting on
    The object of your despair.

It's ugly and nasty,
    Full of filth and slime.
It oozes over you
    Each and every time.

It's something that you can't shake.
    It swallows you up whole.
All at once, it consumes you.
    Lapping at your soul.

It's something that won't let go.
    It won't let you be friendly.
All at once, you're in its grasp,
    The green-eyed monster of—
                  Envy.

WORK

If my best

isn't good enough…

FUCK IT!

$$\frac{\text{WATER}}{\text{ME}}$$

DROWING.

$$\frac{\text{DIRT}}{\text{ME}}$$

SUFFOCATING.

ME

F ^{R}$_{e}$ E

BREATHING.

*The answers to this Rebus puzzle can be found on the last page of book.

Isolation
(A Day in the Life)

I come in early when no one is there.
I leave late after everyone is gone,
      But who cares?
They say I'm too pretty to work in a place like this.
They say I'm too pretty a girl.
      Well…I don't think so.

My radio plays softly so only I can hear. I'm careful that
it disturbs no one. My office cubicle is quiet, and while
around me, I hear my neighboring co-workers. Henry is
on the phone listening intently to a customer. Our
director asks Sam about his vacation. Sam answers, it
was a good one. Then he regales Sam about his vacation
in Hawaii. Debra joins in. Our secretary, Karie, argues
with someone on the phone about a special order.

I need another cup of coffee.

Danny is on the phone discussing last night's game.
My boss is talking to some office managers, laughing
about the same. They talk about the morning commute
and all the snow we've had. In some strange way, I
don't know, I feel a little sad.

Life in the office place has only just begun.
Life in the office place is not much fun.
For others, it's an adventure far away from home.
For me, it's an endless, endless drone.

Looking In from Outside

It's hard living my life in isolation.
It's hard not to get caught up in office conversations.
It's hard not to live vicariously in their lives.
It's hard to know they would rather not hear about
mine.

It's afternoon, and lunchtime has come. Debra calls out
to Sam and Henry. Together, they collect Juan. Karie
has already eaten, or so she says. They call Danny
instead. I know they'll never ask me to join. I've tried a
dozen times, only to be ignored. I grab a small salad and
eat at my desk alone.

Lunch hour seems longer than one. It's snowing again.

The day draws to a close. Danny is furious at a
customer. I try to help. He doesn't hear when I tell of
my success in a similar circumstance. He goes to Debra.
I'm often told I'm not like Debra; she 'thinks like a
man.' I'm obviously outside the communications loop.
Henry is scratching his head again, worrying about a
new car. Sam has an attitude. His one-syllable
answers— "yes"/ "no" are annoying. I overhear Juan
gossiping about me with the rest. I confront him. I joke
that I'll have to start charging .10 cents each time I hear
my name. They laugh. If I had started charging earlier,
I'd be a wealthy woman. I heard them say, in their
defense, "Everyone gets talked about around here."

The price I pay for this privilege is heavy indeed.

Donna Lawrence

Karie gets bossy with the Temp hired to help. The Temp comes to me for advice. I have none. Joanne ignores me with an issue I bring to her. I ask my boss for help. Now Joanne is angry at me. Diane feels I'm unfair to her buddy Joanne. She tells me she'll have nothing more to do with me. I'm not worried. Diane is concerned about her daughter. Joanne can sympathize. What I wouldn't give to be a part of that conversation. Some girl talk would be nice. To make fitting in easier, I think maybe bringing candy to work in individual containers for each of them might brighten their day. I won't let on it's from me.

I'm lonely in the morning.
I'm depressed in the afternoon.
By evening, I have nothing left.
    Maybe I should just shoot myself.

I come home to an empty house. I call my boyfriend. I want to see his face. He has an awful lot to say about his day. I listen. Courtesy dictates that he asks about mine. Relieved to be asked, I start, but it's short-lived. "Get to the point," he says. "I get bored hearing about this stuff." I hang up and go out again. A cheeseburger or a pint of ice cream sounds just fine. My boyfriend calls to apologize. He wants to see a movie. He asks me to pay half. Home from the movie, I place candy in the cutest containers I could find from the shop around the corner. One for each co-worker. I hope they like them. I get ready for another day at the office.

Looking In from Outside

I prepare for bed. I Give Thanks for having a job to
help pay my half for a movie. I consider breaking up
with my boyfriend. I sleep only a few hours. I awake,
sweating from a nightmare.

I come in early when no one is there.
I leave late when everyone is gone,
        But who cares?
They say I'm too pretty to work in a place like this.
They say I'm too pretty a girl.
        Well...I don't think so.

Danny is on the phone discussing another game. My
boss is talking to some office managers, laughing about
the same. They talk about the morning commute and
the amount of snow that's melted. They say it's getting
colder outside and wonder who might have felt it. They
talk about the candy. Who brought it in and why. In
some strange way, I don't know, I let out a grateful sigh.

Life in the office place has only just begun. Life in the
office place is not much fun.
For others, it's an adventure far away from home.
For me, it's an endless, endless drone.

It's hard living my life in isolation.
It's hard not to get caught up in office conversations.
It's hard not to live vicariously in their lives.
It's hard knowing they would rather not hear about
mine,

In isolation.

73

Donna Lawrence

i cry

i cry because of frustration.
i cry because of fear.
i cry because God doesn't hear my prayer.
i cry because i don't know my own mind.

i cry because i don't know what to do.
i cry because i want to be true to myself,
i cry because i don't know who i am.

i shed tears, falling into empty space.
i shed tears that not many see.
i cry still, and sad as it may seem,
i cry for the endless trying not to

cry.

i cry for the child in me.
i cry for the strong woman inside.
i cry for an unknown, uncertain future.
i cry from a broken heart.

i weep no more for this job of mine.
i weep no more over senseless platitudes.
i weep only for me, for myself...

and the courage i must possess.

That Man at Work

I hate this rotten son of a bitch!
Is it surprising that I can't stand his ass?
I don't need his validation,
For this life I've chosen for myself.
Inside or outside my corner of the world
　　　　He Has No Place!

It's not enough for me to sit quietly,
And do the job as best I can.
I refuse to kiss-up to him or anyone.
I make no excuses for being a woman,
A standout performer or
　　　　The Mere Fact That I Exist.

I will not consent to midnight trysts with this
Asshole boss of mine,
Or any co-worker, for that matter.
I will not tolerate harassment,
Discrimination, intimidation.
　　　　Or Acquiesce—In Any Way!

I will stand up against it.
I will speak the unspeakable.
I will put this person in his place,
And to hell with convention.
I will not feel ashamed.
　　　　This works.
　　　　　　　This beats him.

　　　　　　My Superiority.

The Queen Bee

I don't know who she thinks she is,
  Or what it is she's after.
All I know is she's got a bone to pick,
  As if that even matters.

Do I care?
  Yes, I do, and what is it to her?
If sticks and stones can break my bones,
  Then words can surely shatter.

I don't have to take this stuff,
  From her or anyone, no sir!
Let's light the fire and quench the ire,
  For her, we all concur.

That she's too dumb to understand
  I have some amazing gifts.
That of words, sassafras, and lip
  Are at my fingertips.

So, take it on somewhere else,
  Miss dreamed up confection!
Too much air and high derrière,
  Of which I have no affection.

In kissing my behind, she'll never find,
  Where the sun shines is the key.
This stage ain't big enough, you see,
      For a Queen Bee Wannabe.

The Other Side

She smiles brightly, shining into the deep light.

Softly, she laughs and boldly speaks her purpose.
Self-possessed and sure of her direction,
She stands full and proud, with sensuousness and grace.

      I could learn from her.

Unafraid, she continues her next phrasing,
With slight hesitation, until completed thought,
She gestures, then spills, and illuminates us all.

      Her light undoubtedly bright.

She is quite extraordinary, this canvas of perfection.
She does not seem to notice the eyes upon her.
She does not quake or shift from foot or glance.

And yet, I am aware of her dreadlocked hair,
Her black-as-night skin and clear almond-shaped eyes.
Her unaffected attitude of who and what she is,

      Does not diminish her impact but enhances.

Though no great beauty, she silently says she is so.
It bounces off walls, and while I take my leave,
Approaching her outstretched hand, I see how pale,

      And small my palm appears in hers.

I take her hand and hold it firm.
Thanking in my quiet way for I long to be her,
But wish for all the world,

      I had not noticed the colors.

77

Donna Lawrence

Failing in Politics

She's done nothing to anyone.
Not one stone did she throw.
Her character is flawless.
More human than they know.

Therein lies the sin.

Perfection.
We possess it not,
While she comes ever
Closer and taunts.

They raise their hands,
To condemn her.
I watch in silence…

Still.

In horror, I raise my stone,
And ever so slowly…

Thrust.

Why must my stone

Miss the aim

Toward her, who has

Offended me

Not?

Ladder of Success
(Humble Pie)

Gleefully enjoying the triumphant stares.
Gathering my thoughts, I am prepared.
Commanding the stage of just one me.
      Expounding knowledge to the unsuspecting.

Then, one question from the back.
One thrown rock, no dodging the attack
Hits me square in the face, and it hurt....
      Who the hell did I ever think I was?

Confident, I stand strong,
Balanced and degreed,
In my red-soled wrongs,
Polished to a patent sheen.

With one thought, I deflect.
With one quick response,
The record is surely set.
      Unflappable me is who I am.

But wait...the answer is incorrect,

And now strung around my neck,
Is held high for all to see.
The question was thrown to reflect...
      Just who the hell I thought I was.

I fought hard to get here.
I fight hard to stay.
I cower to no one.
I am amazing and brave.
      Who the hell did I ever think I was?

      ...I thought I was me.

Seeking Solace

She cried on the phone today.
She cried and prayed as I listened on the phone that sat
on my shoulder. Telling me of her heart, which broke.
Telling me of her fear and hope.
She cried on the phone today, and I felt her pain.
She ached on the phone with me.
Her voice told me so through wrenching sobs that stole
my heart. It tore through to my weakness, and I
wondered the why of it all.
She cried, and she wept through choking sobs. She
spoke long and loud, trying desperately to find
understanding. Crying to a person who should have
been there to hear but wasn't.
She cried on the phone in vain. She revealed her soul
and her most private thoughts. She showed her true self
and laid bare what she'd hidden all these years. She
wailed and sucked air and cried out to God to anyone
who would listen.
I tried to console,
I tried to reason,
I tried sympathy.
I tried empathy.

I listened for hours and was glad to lend an ear.
Sadly, I could not offer anything more and knew my
shoulders were just NOT broad enough.

I hope in that, and only in that,
I failed her.

False Judgement

Why are we sitting here,
Alone in these halls of injustice?
Waiting for our turn to be heard.
Waiting to be saved
　　　From wrongs undeserved.

To what purpose does this serve?
To be crucified of spirit?
Waiting for retribution or absolution?
Waiting for contributions and restitutions
　　　To satisfy our need for greed.

I, for one, see no justice in this.
Nobility in that arena is lost on me.
I see no resolution to this farce,
This circus of loss within
　　　The power of argument.

I see the futility of effort
With no end in sight.
I see monsters at the gate and door.
I see myself lost forever,
　　　Just to settle a score.

Donna Lawrence

Staring Down Fear

It's never easy, they say,
To confront the worst of us.
It's never easy, they say,
After losing the landslide of trust.

Courage to face the unknown,
Hides but rises when called.
Our Father, Son, and Holy Ghost.
Will never let us fall.

So alone, we face the beast.

We understand the game,
   We stand our ground,
      Our footing sound…
         No shame.
It's hard to face the unknown,
And leave triumphantly.
Hard-fought battles are the bane,
But gives us light to see.

Out there on our own,
Battered and scorned,
We arrive reluctantly.
Standing divided and torn…
      From whom we are thought to be.

Lost and Found

I was audacious once.
I was so pretty and refined.
I had the world by the tail.
I knew the world was mine.

Then things changed...

The world made me look at myself.
The world made me see I wasn't "all that."
The world made me humble and insecure,
I now understand that fact.

I believed what was said of me.
I believed those outlandish lies,
I believed the misguided fantasy,
I think I was truly blind.

Then epiphany...

I found the wreck that was me.
I found the person I had become.
I found the voice that was lost.
I wanted to shout to someone,

And I did...

I no longer listen to the world.
I no longer hide behind false truths.
I am no longer an "IT" to the heralds.

Who am I?

I was never that...

Wild Wind

Watch where the wild wind blows,

Even though you know it's fury.
　　Try to stay ahead of the game.
Be upfront and guarded,
　　Ever watching where you aim.

Ride high the winds of change,
　　And catch the breeze where you can.
For the wind will not be calmed,
　　When you move from destiny's plan.

Beware the lull that in you grows,
　　Stay where the zephyr is at your back.
Be faithful to your purpose and,
　　Hold not the backward track.

The waters of life run swift and deep,
　　Watch carefully as you flow along.
For on the way, you will find,
　　The essence of your soulful song,

　　　　That will soar…
　　　　　　　And soar…
　　　　　　　　　And soar.

PERCEPTION

Water

Never moves against its

own current.

Why should I?

God
gave us two essential
gifts…

Free Will
and a
Reasoning Brain.

I don't think we use
either
one very well.

Doubt

Every man deserves the benefit of the doubt.

Trust, like respect, is universal and must be earned.

It's not until someone gives you a reason to
mistrust that you lose respect.

This is when the seeds of doubt are sown.

Not before.

The Rain
(9/11/01)

It rained in New York today.
Though the sky was blue,
And the sun was high.
It rained in New York today.

It rained in New York today.
The kind of rain I've not seen,
The kind of rain not meant to be.
It rained in New York, anyway.

It rained in New York today.
Though it was ugly and mean,
I could not turn away from looking up.
It rained in New York; how strange.

The clouds were churning in just one spot,
And the gray giants were weeping.
Then the clouds fell down,
And the rain wouldn't stop,
The red rain with flames and leaping.
White dust, gray dust, metal steeping
High upon itself, bits of flesh falling around me,
Sky darkening, cries coming from all directions,
Turning my agony into horror and my flight into
Paralyzed fear and panic, no more rain,
No more rain; I cried for it to stop.
This isn't real; this isn't me running for my life,
Trying to comprehend this terrible,
Awful,
Rain.

All is dust-covered now.
The rain has left a mark.
The memory is clinging.
Sobering and stark.

It rained in New York today.

89

The Heir

I am the heir of courageous men,
Who decided to fight for a country to call their
Own.

I am the heir of hopeful and broken people,
Who decided to stay in a country, not their
Own.

I am the heir of brothers who fought each other,
Who decided their country belonged to them and not
the other to
Own.

I am the heir of heroes who fought in countless battles,
Who decided our sovereignty should be protected and
entirely our
Own.

I am the heir of righteous men and women marching,
Who decided that justice should be equal, and rights
deserved their
Own.

I am the heir of healing mothers,
Who decided that wrongs could be righted, and hearts
uplifted for their
Own.

I am the heir of the air I breathe in this country,
Who decided to recognize that all I am, I owe through
heritage I call my very
Own.

Looking In from Outside

I am the heir, an American, a person from a land of
imperfections,
Who has decided a loud and proud voice can cite
exceptional triumphs.
Who will not be silenced.
Whose words will not be suppressed.
Whose religious beliefs will not be scoffed.
Who will stand for justice when injustice is rife. Who
will fight with sweat and blood for the soul of a nation,
in pursuit of the sweet, sweet bounty that freedom has
brought,
As God is my witness.

For the price of liberty is too high a price to pay,
If we lose the country, I am proud to call my
Own.

I Am Heir.

What It Takes

It takes courage to write anything these days.
It takes courage to say what's on your mind.
It takes courage to chase your fears away.
It takes effort to turn water into wine.

I don't have a lot of courage,
And I don't have a lot of time.
I don't have a lot of grudges,
But I do have a mountain to climb.

I only have the conviction to seek the truth,
As I hold pencil to paper.
I only have a voice to raise the roof,
I hope they appreciate the labor.

It takes courage to speak up and out loud.
It takes courage to be able to bend.
It takes courage to stand up and be proud.
It takes courage to be counted and then,

If it takes all I have, I will do this,

...if just to feel free again.

The Majesty of Nature

Storms beat around me as I stand tall.
Grasses bend at the will of the wind,
  …And I do not feel small.

Buffeted and churned are the seeds of grain,
That feeds our empty souls,
  …And I am born again.

Batten and gusseted we seek shelter,
Unable to weather the oncoming,
  …And I, the only detector.

I am not afraid of nature's wrath.
I am not cowed by the maelstrom.
I will not succumb to the unyielding lash.
I will stand despite the tantrum,

  For I know the reason why.

Noises cease, and all is calm.
Amazing has been the outcome,
  …And I alone unharmed.

Storms will rise, and winds will wail,
For a purpose so divine that
Washes away the tainted veil,
  That nourishes the soil of time.

Losing Ground

The man on the edge of the cliff is losing his mind.
The man on the edge of the cliff
Is ready to cash it in because "It's all much, too much."

The man on the edge is in pain.
The man on the edge is lost.
The man on the edge is naive.

He believes in the Father, Son, and Holy Ghost.
He believes in the goodness of people.
He believes in fate and is a decent man.

He also believes in the Tooth Fairy.

What he doesn't know is that:
The Tooth Fairy is a family member who loves you.
Santa Claus is the surprise you get on Christmas morning.
The Easter Bunny is the good feeling that grows in your
heart.

Life is not fair.

The free lunch, the free ride,
The free admission must be paid,
Sooner or later.

And still, he stands.
So close to the edge
He smiles, then…
Topples.

I cry out to him,
But he doesn't hear me.
I reach out to him,
As he pulls away…

If only he could have turned away from this edge.
If only he could have turned his back to the cliff.
If only he could have realized that hope was in the
Turning around…

The Mighty Fall

Much of this, I don't understand.
　　Much of this is out of hand.
Much is taken from our plan.
　　Mighty is fallen this one man.

Man is made of flesh and bone,
　　Far from those he has left at home.
Pushed and pulled, he gained his feet,
　　Only to be taken by defeat.

Courageously, we stood by his side,
　　Praising all that is left behind.
Moving as one, we sang his song,
　　Daring to stand forever strong.

All too soon, we toss aside,
　　Achievements that are brought to mind.
We care not for the fight he has led,
　　Or the sacrifices left unsaid.

Unfair the way we treat him thus.
　　Time is time we treasure much.
Throwing him out is just our way?
　　We will find someone for another day.

Much of this, I don't understand.
　　Too much of this is out of hand.
So much of this is too much to take....
　　Time is time—
　　　　　We must awake.

The Rising

Beware the rising people.
    Those who sit silently by.
Those who wait and watch in wonder,
    Their patience in short supply.

Beware the rising people.
    Those who always contemplate.
Those who understand the noisome.
    Those who respect the debate.

These are those who will come calling,
    When the winds of change are nigh.
These are those no longer stalling,
    Who walk with head held high.

Beware the rising people.
    Take care to gird your soul.
The knowing and all-seeing,
    Comes for those outside the fold.

Beware the rising people.
    The ones who will take charge.
As they push forward without warning
    Growing ever and ever large…

                    Beware the rising people.

Times Up

I heard on the radio,
    That I must get home.
I said, "He's a liar,
    His pants are on fire."
But this is no joke,
    I believe there is hope.
I've got to get with it.
    I just have to kick this.

Can't get on an airplane,
    Or hop on the next train.
Can't see while I'm sleeping,
    I simply can't explain.
Can we speak on the telephone?
    Oh no, you're not at home.
Don't know what I'm doing.
    Who am I fooling?

Pointing fingers won't last.
    This is a moment,
I must get past.
    What do I have to do?

Check into the front desk,
    This is my best guess.
Jump into the shower,
    You know it has power.
Make sure that I'm clean,
    This sickness is very mean.
Now I'm just tired,
    Feel like I'm wired.

I'm running on time.
    I'm running on borrowed time.
I'm running on time.
        I'm running out of time.

Donna Lawrence

Words Unsaid

Hey Ruth, what's the truth? What's wrong with the
world today? They say...we'll pay.
I don't know about you, but what's
　　　To do?

I'm trying to find the truth here.
To find the words they say,
　　　And they don't.

Hey Ruth, I'm scared. Will we see another light?
Can we find...another way?
I don't know about you, but something
　　　Ain't right.

We have the RIGHT to know.
We have the RIGHT to fight.
We have the RIGHT to choose.
We even have the RIGHT to die!

　　　BUT

I'm TRYING to find the TRUTH here.
To find the words they say...
　　　And they don't.

　　　　　They just won't.

I Miss People

I DON'T KNOW ABOUT YOU, but I miss people. I miss people who care about each other. I miss people who share with each other. I miss people who see skin color and just don't give a damn.

I miss people who take action when action is needed. I miss people who get angry when appropriate, holding nothing back. I miss people who aren't blind and know what's what. I miss people who speak the truth told uncut. I miss people who never give an inch. I miss people who are hard to convince.

I miss people who mind.

I miss people who empathize and commiserate. I miss people who have generous spirits. I miss people who lend a helping hand. I miss people who understand. I miss people who tell me I'm wrong. I miss people who sing lovely songs. I miss people who look after us, especially our youth. I miss grandmas and grandpas, even if some are missing a tooth.

I miss people who are young, old, and wise.

I miss people who love out loud. I miss people who cry in public. I miss people who laugh with abandon. I miss people who are alone. I miss people who stay at home. I miss people who trash talk and play on words. I miss people who are ugly and true. I miss people who are beautiful too. I miss people who walk, talk, and dress funny. I miss people who don't have a lot of money. I miss people who have a lot of things.

I miss people who have gone away.

I miss people who love their families with fierceness. I miss people who yell at taxis. I miss people who want to make others happy. I miss people who love to smile. I miss people who stay for a while. I miss people who are dog and cat people and love all animals just the same. I miss people who are movers, shakers, and even candlestick makers. I miss people who love to teach. I miss people who hustle for glory and fame. I miss people with unusual names. I miss people from other countries. I miss people who want to make a better life. I miss people who stand up for their rights. I miss people who believe in a higher being.

I miss people who pray.

I miss people for many reasons, almost too many to name. I miss people for all the right reasons, come what may. I miss people because I miss people. I miss all the lovely, unlovely ways of humans who make life worth living and keep me going from day to day.

I miss people.

An Unconventional Metaphor

I LOVE MY HOUSE.

I like the different rooms and the cohesive way one room flows into the other. I like the different kinds of furniture and how they are placed inside each area and room. I love the way the light plays off one wall that, in turn, illuminates the opposite walls, which showcase their beauty depending on the time of day. I can mark the time by the placement of this light, which brings me joy. I love the different types of frames that frame my artwork and photos of those I love, particularly those who have meant a lot to me and passed on. I like the vaulted ceilings that hover at the perfect height above my head and carry sound so perfectly. I love the way it protects me and makes me feel safe. I like the feel of each room and the different energy each one brings to my spirit. The setup done intentionally for that particular purpose is pure bliss.

My bathroom is an oasis of peace and full of different fragrances that calm my soul and ease my mind. My study contains books by various authors, fiction and non-fiction, and informational resources. They mark the time in life and my travels, all different cultures, and memories that are simply wonderful. The exercise equipment is well-used and stands as sentinels to remind me of my commitment to get and staying healthy. I would change nothing to make anything in my house the same.

The different colors, textures, and lights make my house a home. Different types of food in the fridge, different types of jewelry, clothing, and fabrics; it's all good. Outside, my garden is blooming with various flowers and herbs that give off a lovely fragrance when in full bloom. I love to sit outside and watch different types of birds chirp and visit from time to time to eat the bird seeds I've put out for them. I love watching the different trees move and sway with the wind and feeling the soft breeze on my face. It is relaxing to be surrounded by many different things that bring joy to my sense of being.

Differences.

I wonder how many notice the number of times I mentioned the word 'different'? Not many, I would guess, and maybe that's okay. It's the differences that give us variety in life. It's the differences that make life interesting. It's cliché to say life would be boring without differences, but I want to put it out there to make a point, as subtle as it is. Our differences make us unique. And it is those differences that create harmony—if that makes sense. Our differences make us curious, which helps us learn more about each other, life, and different ideas. We need each other to bring enrichment to our inner houses.

I hope we aren't missing this fact.

My house is distinctly different from the others, and I like it; it's not cookie-cutter. That may not be okay for some, who am I to judge. But, just like me, it's different. My neighbors are as diverse as the shoes in my closet, and I like that, too. Not that I'm equating people with shoes, but I think you get the point. In fact, I love this aspect of my neighborhood, which is why I live here.

I wouldn't like someone pointing out all the differences in my house, admonishing me for not wanting the same color scheme, photo frames, type of food, etcetera, ad infinitum. That would make me feel bad and wonder what was wrong with *me* that I couldn't embrace sameness. The pull to be like everyone else is sometimes too great to ignore! Before long, after changing everything to "sameness," I would be miserable, not to mention physically unhealthy, leading me to question my mental health – believe me, and more than a little pissed at myself. I would resent the person for shaming me into redoing my home, not to mention the expense of doing such a thing! I'd work like hell to change it back; an expensive lesson, to be sure, but one I highlight here as a not-so-subtle point in social interaction.

Differences.

Let's celebrate it. Let's live it and embrace it fully. We did this subconsciously not long ago, and all was relatively fine. To hear someone talk about our differences on a daily basis is annoying. 'Yes, I know we're different. So what!? Now leave us alone… *please.*' In fact, some of us might want to say this in not-so-gentle terms.

I love being different—the Ying and Yang of balance. I love diversity and all the rest of it, and it works perfectly together in my house and everyday life; thank you very much.

I love my house and all its differences.

FYI: The number of times the word 'different' is mentioned = Who cares?

Simply: AMERICA

America. A. merica. Ahhh merika.

HOWEVER YOU SAY THIS WORD, it has the ring of something magical. I'm only speaking for myself here, but I do believe most of us, and those of the world, think of America as the shining beacon that beckons: Look at me, Be like me. We are good. We are fiercely righteous. We have overcome and are still standing because of our faults. We have prospered. We are strong. Much has been written along these lines, and I understand if others don't share these sentiments. But I also understand we are the one nation the world looks to for hope, faith, and freedom.

We are what freedom means.

Other nations see us much like that popular person we all longed to be in high school. The one we wanted to emulate because we thought they had so much. If only we could get close enough to breathe that rarified air, we hoped some of their luster would rub off on us. Then we, too, would be as wonderful and great. That's what we thought.

But there's another side.

That person has flaws we don't see. We don't think about faults because, to us, that person is otherworldly and

105

above us, just beyond our reach. We fail to see that those flaws make that person who they are. The nose may not be perfectly shaped, but it fits the face. The teeth may be slightly crooked, but if straightened, it might alter what makes them who they are. How they look matters, which we accept unconsciously. These physical or mental changes would alter how they hold, see, and conduct themselves in the world around them. We may see something we hadn't seen before, which might make us uncomfortable. Unless done for medical reasons, these changes could very well upset our core beliefs in that person. Trust comes into question.

We all long for perfection, but imperfections are good. No one is perfect, nor should they be. No nation is perfect, nor should it be. This is what makes America great. Never one to flaunt our assets; they just exist. Never one to throw our weight around, we just assist. Never one to sit back and let things happen to us; we make things happen for us. We make ourselves better, and the world prospers from that effort. We strive for this, and in most cases, this is true.

That's what America used to be, and I think that ideal still lives on.

I've heard it said that Americans and those in Western civilizations are the only ones in battle who fight with a conscience. They do what they must but live with the pain of what they've had to do in combat. It weighs heavy because of the innate religious belief of 'do unto others as we would have done to ourselves.'

The states that comprise America are united and somewhat different than other nations. Yet, we are no different than those who want what we want or what we have. Our ideologies may differ, but our needs are all the same. Maybe we have more, or perhaps the grass just looks greener over here than from there. I don't know. But whatever it is, people still long to be part of what we have, and the desire to be in our land still drives them here, regardless of our faults.

Our imperfections make us great, not perfect. Our acknowledgments of our failings keep us strong. Our belief that we *can* do better keeps us courageous. Land of the free. Home of the brave. Love or hate us, I am proud of who we *were*, who we've *become*, and who we *are*.

I just pray we keep it that way.

AMERICA

Bull-Sh*t

YOU KNOW THE WORLD is full of so much bullshit! It is really pathetic. How much of this can one person take? I mean, let's get real. Bullshit jobs, bullshit people, bullshit politics, bullshit laws, bullshit bills, bullshit news, bullshit cars, clothes, housing, relatives, bullshit, bullshit, bullshit!

There is so much of it we don't see it.

We don't even recognize our own bullshit because we've grown accustomed to its smell. Our senses have become sensitized to the overwhelming repugnance that we don't recognize that we're dying here. Choking in our own mess. Evolving to become complacent automatons making it through one day at a time. Mundane, stupid, pathetic puppets of life and leisure. Wanting to be led, needing to be told where to go, what to do and not do.

The America we thought we knew needs rethinking.

The 'We,' we thought we knew. The 'I' needs to be rethought.

I don't know about you, but I feel the urge to break free. To run away from the filth and decay to fresh fields of clover, flowers, and sunshine. To warm green grass nourished by rich soil. To run with the wind roaring through my hair and clouds soaring from above. To let the sunlight bask me in its glory.

Looking In from Outside

Ahhhh!

The pure soul-cleansing joy of it. And then, by and by, I'd lie down and sleep—a profoundly peaceful and quiet sleep. No dreams, just rest. Awakened, refreshed, and empty—drained. The drink of mental peace is amazing. Just me and God. I invite you to join in, too, just you and your own commune with the One higher than yourself. Aliens—maybe? Whatever.

Just be and become whole and ready to be filled again. Renewed.
I wish I could stay on forever and ever in Shangri-la, but I can't. I'd have to return after a time. Instead of daydreaming and day-tripping my life away, I would need to make a living. Try as I might, I can't escape the mess I live in. But, returning from nirvana, I'd be better prepared to see, smell, and recognize what my life has become and somehow try to turn it around.

You never know. It may just take one person, then another, and another until finally, we can all come together to bring about truth. Not bullshit. Not complacency. Not degradation. None of the filth we have accepted.

Who needs it?

I don't. Never have, for you see, we all know that *bullshit is there*. We've just accepted it as entertainment, basically.

A callous form of show that, after a while, numbs us. In numbing us, it makes us less aware.
Cleansing of the soul is a wonderful thought indeed.

I may be wrong for all I know. I'm tired of the never-ending, ever-winding, day-to-day trudge and drudge of living. The need of waiting and never getting. The changes and arranges we find we must do each and every day. What a chore. What a waste.

Now, if I could just find that meadow I was speaking of.

ᨑ LOSS ᨒ

Donna Lawrence

WHY?

The

Universal Question

of Man.

Simply Sorry
(To Rescue a Friendship)

I think the world of you.
You might not know this, but I do.
As a brother and a friend,
I know you love me too.

Sometimes, words said in haste,
Can cause sadness and pain.
I never meant to hurt you,
For there is nothing to be gained.

Except to say I'm sorry,
For speaking out of turn.
I hope you understand,
This has been a lesson learned.

You are family to me and
There is nothing I wouldn't do,
To have you understand
How much I respect and care,
About you.

Losing a Child

What can one say at the loss of a child?
  What can one do at the loss of a smile?
Any loss is tragic; we're doomed from the start.
  How can you manage pain that comes from the
heart?

How does one continue when the day suddenly stops?
  Where does one go when the other shoe drops?
We tell ourselves it's not fair, this can't be so, and NO!
  How can we see tomorrow when the other door has
closed?

What do we tell our friends who sadly watch?
  How do we deal with the sorrow this day has
wrought?
Numb from pain we move through each day,
  Hoping all tears will be washed away.

Reminders of yesterday and days to come,
  Do they fade as slowly as the setting sun?
But twilight remains, and it is here we go,
  To grieve the loss that has brought us low.

What can one say at the loss of a child?
  What can one do at the loss of a smile?
Tho' we carry on as best we can,
  Keeping memories close
              …For a loss unplanned.

Lay Your Heavy Burdens
(On the Loss of a Beloved Nephew)

Throw away your sword into the thorns,
You will not need it now.
As the wind lifts you above the horns,
Banish demons from your brow.

No need to worry about tomorrow,
Put down the hefty trowel.
What is left is but sweet sorrow,
Resting heavy upon the bough.

Long are gone the wretched days,
Of worry and misgivings.
Long are gone the wretched ways,
Now left among the living.

Reach out your hand and touch the light,
Of glory and forever.
Turn away from what is left behind,
For you will see it never.

Lay down the load that was unplanned,
It has finally come to rest.
Sleep now, my prince, and understand,
That you have done your best.

Walk softly through the open door—
And know that you were blessed.

115

Donna Lawrence

Loss of a friend

My soul took flight last night,
To journey with a friend.
A friend I had not seen in years,
To wander without end.

We walked on clouds above the moon.
We spoke earnestly and long.
We talked of nothing and everything,
Of unrealized dreams and songs.

All too soon, the visit's done,
Imagine my surprise.
When once I woke to discover,
They'd vanished before my eyes.

I do not mourn because I know,
Whenever I'm in need,
I close my eyes, and I'm with them,
To smile sweet memories

    …Of days and friends gone by.

A Now Silent Voice
(For Loss of a Beloved Uncle)

You pulled me off the wall and swept me off my feet,
then exclaimed,
>> "Look, y'all, I'm dancing with my niece!"

Those simple steps you taught me well have held me
fast today.
>> And since that time, you've been my friend,
>> and never have I strayed.
For an unsure girl in a mixed-up world of where I stood
apart,
>> Your guidance sure and words endured, are
>> kept here in my heart.

Your voice surreal and with notes of steel, you carried
the starry-eyed,
>> Generosity you bestowed on many as they
>> cried.
To touch your hair but, with a withering stare, a torch
to burn the heart,
>> I stood behind and often pined when I would
>> get my start.

Through many years and bitter tears, you've shared with
me your plight.
>> Your hopes and dreams and storied telling of
>> demons in the night.
I hurt for you, and with you, too, I championed your
fight,
>> But all too well, we tell the tale of vigils,
>> wrongs, and rights.

As princes ride their gallant steeds with swords
appointed high,
        Then downward plod as home they trod for
        sorrows are but nigh.
Your guiding light that shown so bright has dimmed a
bit today,
        Sleep well, my knight, sleep my uncle…
            Where you forever lay.

Mysteries

With its last dying breath,
The swan sings its
Most beautiful
song.

Trees are most glorious,
When their leaves
Are dying in
The fall.

Salmon swim upstream
To give life,
Not knowing it's the end
Of their own.

Soldiers go off to war,
Then lose their lives
selflessly,
So far away from home.

Man is given many years,
While some pets receive fifteen.
In those years of unconditional love
They often die alone.

Why is it these most unselfish,
Beautiful acts often occur
At the end of
Spectacular feats?

❧ Reflection ❧

I am

awestruck by the

beauty and magic

that

maturity brings.

Short and Sweet

I've been smart.
I've been bright.
I've been stupid.
I've been right.

I've seen it all,
Or so I thought.
      But,
I never thought
      I'd rue the day…
         that I met you.

On My Wings

How I wish I could fly
    Away from the noise and pain,
To a place where I'm free again.

How I wish I could see
    Beyond the heartache and tears,
To a place where there is no fear.

On my wings of hope,
    On my wings of faith,
On my wings of love.
    I will sing again.
I will live again.
    I will do again.

On wings
        …that are my very own.

Being Home

It was back home,
    I dreamed of being.
It was Kentucky,
    I dreamed of being.

Back to the warm
    Bright sunshine.
Back to the lost
    Memories of time.

It was green, lush, and promising.
    It was bright, warm, and whole.
It was just the amount I needed.
    It was the feeling of being home.

So, it's back home,
    I dream of being.
It was Kentucky,
    I dream of being.

Back to simple
    Quiet times.
Back to feeling
    My life was fine.

Owning Me

I've found my song again.
    The notes are high and clear.
Everything is fresh and new,
    And I feel young, my friend.

The sun is brighter than starlight.
    The air is crisp and clean.
I'm walking ten feet off the ground.
    Heck, I feel like a Queen.

I can't begin to imagine my life,
    If I felt any better than now.
I can't blame it on anything else,
    Gone is the furrow from my brow.

It's me I've found and embraced.
    It's me I've surrendered to.
My goodness, all this time,
    It couldn't be more true.

I like myself again.
    I adore just who I am.
I was there all along.
    My life no longer a sham.

All is right with the world.
    My center of being...
                        Just me.

Lost and Found

How was I to know,
I was being missed?
How was I to know,
I was your secret wish?

I wandered around
Lost and beaten.
Never knowing that
Love was calling my name.

And then you found me.
Quietly you searched,
Not daring to ask directly,
The question of your thirst.

So little time.
So much to say.
Where do we start,
To mend our broken hearts?

How was I to know,
I was being missed?
How was I to know,
I was your secret wish?
   But you found me.

The Beauty of Things

I've seen blooming flowers in a full moon's rise.
I've seen shooting stars and wished on them, too.
I've seen eclipses in the heavens and towering
    thunderclouds
Those gigantic billowing wonders against a crystal clear
        sky of blue.

I've seen human faces of every hue.
I've seen leaves of trees in every shade in autumn.
I've seen thoroughbreds with shiny manes.
Even cats and dogs wear silken fur-like coats of
    vibrancy,
        so awesome.

I've seen the gorgeous beauty of the male and female.
I've seen the creative works of tailored clothes.
I've seen the strut of confidence as it sauntered on
    its way.
The kindness of others on full display is amazing
        as it grows.

I've seen the joy on new mothers' and fathers' faces.
I've seen the smile of a child's joy when tickled gently.
I've seen the long embrace of lovers with kisses deep
    and sweet.
Love is always beautiful when displayed, often and long,
        however incidentally.

I've seen green rolling hills and soaring mountains.
I've seen snow on the highest peaks.
I've seen deserts vast and barren.
I've seen some amazingly beautiful things
        that silently speak.

But in the early dawn of new sunrises,
Or the setting of the sun at the end of the day,
I am left breathless...

        For only God can paint the sky that color.

Evenings Closure

Sounds grow silent as evening draws near,
    A calmness settles over my wanton fears.
I sigh to welcome the closing of day,
    Whose beauty takes my breath away.

Red, Blue, and gold line the evening sky
    As darkness moves the sun to lie,
But steady to rise at birds' sweet song,
    Heralding another day to chase along.

Until then, my mind will take the time
    To relish this soulful, meandering rhyme,
That stills me in the coolness of this night,
    As weariness is tucked away from sight.

Sad are we to meet the end
    Of daily grinds that wane again,
To blessed sighs and sweet relief,
    And early mornings rising…

        …After resting at peace.

Hope

As the sun rises on the dawn of a brand-new year, I am struck by many thoughts. The most prominent one is hope.

Hope for the preservation of our nation.
Hope in us turning more toward God for guidance.
Hope that the decency man has for his fellow man will be abundant. Hope that our tomorrow will be better than our yesterday.
Hope that we recognize our blessings and appreciate the beauty in all things.
Hope that when called upon, we will be at our best, especially in the face of adversity.

I hope that God's greatest gifts, a cognitive reasoning brain, and free will, will be fully utilized to help us stand together for what is right and evenly measured.

And I hope that these mere wishes are attainable goals that will see us through to the next year and beyond.

Be Still

ENJOY THE QUIET. It is whisper-soft…

These days, it seems that even our religious belief in walking by faith and not by sight has been upended. In secular life, we need proof to believe. In that, we walk by sight and not by faith. Just because there is no physical evidence of Moses doesn't mean he didn't exist. We need to believe in something, and faith will get us there.

So be still for a moment.

Absorb the quiet and languish in the beauty of silence. Throw away worry and pain. Leave thoughts for tomorrow at tomorrow's door; they are not for today. All will be well regardless of what may happen. Satan has no place when Jesus is on the right hand of God. It is all in God's hands anyway.

So be still for a moment.

Enjoy the soft, rippling thoughts of sunshine and light. Blessed is he who understands God's word and loves Jesus. Stand strong in faith, knowing that there is nothing we can't withstand. Inhale deeply, hold onto each breath long enough to fill the lungs and slowly exhale, feeling the tension of the day's stress release.

So be still for a moment.

Just a moment in time is all that's needed to reset. Just a moment in time is all that's needed to unwind—just a moment of quiet to find peace. The quiet is whisper soft.

Be still.

Seasons

Once upon a time, there lived a man, or so the saying
      goes.
He lived, worked, and played among the aging stones.
How strange it seemed the change started without
      Him being aware.
How strange it seemed the change started without
      Him having a care.

Once upon a time, a wizened owl lived, or so the saying
      goes.
He watched the man idly by perched among the stones.
How strange it seemed the change occurred without
      Him wondering why.
How strange it seemed the change occurred without
      Noticing the shifting sky.

Once upon a time seems so long ago, or so the saying
      goes.
The man, the owl are long gone now but thus remain
      the stones.
How strange it seemed that time untouched the turning
      Of the tide.
How strange it seemed that all the while we lived and so
      We die.

Seasons.

131

Reflections

IN THE DAY-TO-DAY NESS of everyday life, I think we forget to take in the amazing gift that God has given us— to live as fully and love as long as we can, for tomorrow is not promised.

It's about smelling the proverbial roses along the way.

In other words, enjoy life as fully as we can in every way possible. Oh, and watch out for the thorns. They really aren't that bad.

They, too, have their purpose.

Looking In from Outside

I live my life among ghosts.
I live among those whom I've loved and lost,
  And gone on before me.
I rage against the life I could have had.
I rage against the jealousy that has kept me in a cage,
  A captive voyeur of life that I can't escape.

I live among those who will not accept me.
I live with memories that I cannot shake,
  And traumas too hard to erase.
I rage against those who have hurt me.
I rage against the misunderstood ramblings,
  I've tried to convey but can't quite.

I love looking into the lives of others.
I live wondering about the many jokes,
  Told at my expense.
I rage against the nature of thoughtlessness.
I rage against the insensitive common,
  Who thinks nothing of slinging dirt.

I live alone in isolation.
I live in the white light of loneliness,
  My pure existence.
I rage against an unfair life.
I rage against my cosmic fate,
    Craving color.

ଈ AUTHOR'S WALK ଓ

I

Walk empty shores
alone.

Always.

Creative Lament

Words upon words roll through my mind,
The process is never-ending.
Time and time again, I write the verse.
Time and time again, I see the narrative,
      And pray it doesn't get worse.

It drives me crazy as if it could,
The Creative will not be defied.
My room is festooned with scribbles.
If I cease then slowly will release,
      This endless need to quibble.

But I can't—

If hard to find, then great is the time,
The enjoyment I'll never deny.
From writing and rhyming, I am remiss,
From singing, drawing, and minding
      My own business.

It is my fate to create and see,
The dancing images in my head.
To view it unfold and marvel so bold,
Making the intangible something
      to behold.

Unlike Sisyphus, I gladly push the muse uphill…
      And accept my quest undone.

The Crosses We Bear

LATELY, I AM REMINDED of the crosses we bear. In my opinion, some crosses are incredibly light, while others are heavy indeed. The cross I speak of is borne out of guilt, regret, unrequited love, shame, unfulfilled dreams... you know the rest. It's something we have longed to do but never did, something we have always wanted to achieve but couldn't, some measure of mettle we've wanted but lacked the desire to attain, some shortcoming to overcome, but for some reason could not.

Crosses can be heavy, but I think it's all relative.

Some people meet challenges in life and forge ahead regardless of the task. Some people don't give a rip about the difficult path that lies ahead and soldiers onward. Some people see mountains as mere steppingstones, which are nothing for them to go around or climb over, metaphorically speaking. Some people can cope better than others, and I commend them.

Others of us struggle. We struggle because we want the best. We struggle because we want our lives to be as perfect as can be. We struggle because we can't accept the mediocre. We struggle because we feel that others have let us down. We struggle because we just don't want to believe...in ourselves. We struggle because we cannot accept that life *is* a struggle. But it doesn't have to be. As they say, 'we must play the cards we're dealt' and play as best we can.

But how do we accept the day-to-dayness of 'struggle?'

137

We can start now. We can accept that we are blessed in so many ways. That is if we choose to accept this perspective. Life is hard and unfair in many respects, but neither is it dreadful in other aspects. For instance, here are a few things I feel are good to consider:

There's no need to feel guilty over imagined wrongs; apologize and move on.

Life's too short for regrets. If you know you've done your best, don't dwell on what should/could have been(s). Your best may not have been *great*, but at least you tried, and that's what's best.

Never live your life for others. Be your authentic self and best self. Love yourself and embrace who you are. Once you do, it's surprising how others will come to you.

Maybe the love of your life just never materialized or wasn't meant for you. If he/she were, you wouldn't have to wonder, now, would you?

Never allow someone to make you feel ashamed; it's a sin for them to do so and not for you to accept. Guilty maybe, but *ashamed*—never!

It's good to have dreams for a better life. Never let them go; if they're not fulfilled, at least you *could* dream when so many do not, cannot, or will not. Work as hard as you can for the rewards you seek. It may not mean a six-figure salary, but it gives purpose to your life, making life worthwhile and worth living.

These are just a few ways of accepting our lot in life. Perspective is everything. Of course, all of this is easier said than done, right? In that regard, I'm reminded of a bible passage which states:

> ...it is well for a man to eat and drink and enjoy all the fruits of his labor under the sun during the limited days of the life which God gives him; for this is his lot. Any man to whom God gives riches and property, and grants power to partake of them, so that he receives his lot and finds joy in the fruits of his toil, has a gift from God. For he will hardly dwell on the shortness of his life because God lets him busy himself with the joy of his heart. ~ Ecclesiastes 5:17-18.

So why am I telling you this?

I say this as a gift. Remember, all is not as it seems. As forlorn and unhappy we may feel, at least that feeling lets us know we're alive. Alive to live another day to make things happen, improve our outlook, and accept that this is all we get sometimes. If we get more, it's a blessing; until then, enjoy and make the most of what we have.

Our Lord, Jesus Christ, was given to us by the grace of God to die for our sins. It's good to remember that He carried His cross because it was time for Him to do so, and so shall ours be. Due to perseverance, a positive outlook, and acceptance, our travail will not be long once we've laid down our cross.

A cross is not a curse. It's a reminder that life is meant to be lived with all its joys and sorrows. So, I say, step

139

Donna Lawrence

bravely into all the wonderful tomorrows to come with gratitude and grace. Know that the cross we bear is only that which becomes lighter in weight as we move through the life we have chosen to live.

Gaining from Tribulations

WHEN DID I GROW OLD 'ER? Some of us lament. When was it I realized that for every five steps I take forward, there are three I take back? When did the words persevere, grit, fortitude, endure, and overcome become a mantra I recite each morning when I wake? Rest, relax, don't lose heart; this too will pass, and yes, tomorrow is another day; these words seem so obviously clichéd.

Cement is a hard substance that weeds tend to break. Shattering the notion that strength, against willfulness, is an achievement. The ability to see past tomorrow has its merit.

So, moving forward, I must.

If I stop, I might fall. Failure is not an option. Gaining from tribulation is something I must gloat about. I take with glee the ability to rise above my trials. Winds may blow, waters may rise, fires might rage, lifting smoke to the sky, but I remain.

Until my last breath, I will hold firm to the thought that standing strong, unbending, yet soft is the way to plant myself, chart my path, and leave a legacy of just being who I am.

Donna Lawrence

The Elusive Dream of Sleep

THE WRITING WORRIES of authorship can wreak havoc on sleep. I remember a time when I slept like a rock. Falling asleep was never my problem. *Staying* asleep, well, that's a whole 'nother matter nowadays.

When we were small, there was very little to worry about. We took naps all the time—this was maybe the effect of expending too much energy from eating sugar, but still, it was something we did. Sleep was something that just happened. No thought. No angst about it. Just sleep.

Slumber these days has become an elusive son of a gun. I could wax semi-poetic here and say something clever, like "elusive as a scurrying cockroach" or some such, but I ain't gonna. Some days, I walk by my bed and dread lying down at night to find sleep. I don't call it a "bed" anymore. I call it "that damn thing." Sometimes I sleep better elsewhere, like the couch or chair, than in that damn thing.

The idea of fighting wakefulness is an activity not made for lying in bed—if you know what I mean. I hope that makes sense.

That elusive dream of sleep. In other words, the thought or idea of slumber is never far from my mind, let me tell ya. Oh no! It's so bad that I have dreams of sleeping when I do sleep! The nightmarish vision of *dreaming* you're asleep brings images of Saint Peter at the Pearly Gates. I don't know about you, but I'm not keen on visiting those gates any time soon. Thank you very much.

I'm starting to believe that blessed, peaceful sleep is an elusive dream and a thing of the past.

Getting older brings on aches and pains we didn't have before. We have worries that keep us tossing and turning at night. Did I mention writing? Heck, there is a whole industry of sleep aids, pillows, mattresses, and supplements designed to help with this issue. Television commercials are full of suggestions begging us to try something new, like a cuddle buddy pillow or one shaped like an angel wing for neck support.

So, I don't think it's my imagination that there is a problem with sleep these days?

I've been asked, "Have you ever…" on many occasions, such as meditation? Yes. Scary. Sorry to say, but I thought I'd conjured something back from the dead. Medication? Yes. Didn't do a thing for me. Warm milk? Yes. But without chocolate in it, I don't understand the point. Try exhausting yourself with an aerobic workout during the day so you can sleep better at night? Yes. Did I mention aches and pains? Lowering the thermostat to 67 degrees or less? Yes. Nearly froze to death! Reading a book? Yes. But my own is not exactly sleep-inducing.

"Have you ever tried watching ASMR?" Wait. What? Most of these videos are very well done, and some are informational or downright comical. Most make sense to others; they just don't seem to work for me.

So, what to do?

Well, for one thing, I'll stop cursing my bed. It's not the bed's fault I can't find sleep. The other thing is to stop looking for sleep. I think it might be better to let sleep find me. Relax as much as possible and accept the process when it comes. Then, nestle in the beautiful slumber that sleep can bring.

Here's hoping for the best.

Writing World

WRITERS DEVELOP A NARRATIVE that takes the reader through the uncharted territory of the author's imagination, where thoughts and dreams are brought to reality when written on the page. Writing is a lonely business and a prospect that is hard to embrace. In this state of solitude, writing can also bring about all manner of insecurities, doubt, and isolation. In today's climate, ideas do not flow as freely as they should. The creative process is hindered by concerns that shouldn't be, such as censorship and the like.

To combat this, one of the many things I like to do is embrace the process and immerse myself in the story and the message I want to convey. I try not to worry about the many constraints placed on the process, likes, and dislikes, and concentrate on the authenticity of the whole. What I mean by "the whole" is the writing process itself, starting at the beginning and imagining the end result once completed.

Taking an idea or premise of a story and seeing it to its conclusion is wonderful; constraints should not get in the way of expression.

To prepare mentally for the task, I make sure there is a quiet place to dwell while working. Sitting in my study, surrounded by books, journals, and reference materials, I am reminded of the job at hand. A quiet water feature gurgles and serves as background music for the day. A cup of hazelnut-flavored coffee never fails to wipe the cobwebs of sleep from my mind.

Then it's go time.

I also set a time to get up and stretch, go for a walk, or call a friend. It breaks up the monotony of sitting for so long. Tea in the afternoon is also a welcome change and something to look forward to as the day progresses.

For me, distractions are only there to provide inspiration. A knock on the door from a girl selling cookies reminds me of a time and place when I did the same. I ask myself what her life must be like, what she will become, and what obstacles she will need to overcome. It's then that my imagination takes off—just like that.

I've heard that stage actors, like all creatives such as writers, painters, and poets, have lives always full of drama. Chaos constantly reigns, and they're never satisfied with the mundane. They need that kind of "fuel" to feed the creative process. How else will they draw upon the muse to create and inspire?

Well, I don't know about *all* that.

What I do know is that peace brings about introspection, and for me, that is where creativity lies. Going about life and observing the day-to-day is enough to inspire most of us.

Looking In from Outside

As lonely as the writing profession can be, I'll take it any day over chaos. Trust me. In the lone introspection of writing, there's no other place I'd rather be.

And I wouldn't have it any other way.

Rudeness!

IT'S SEPTEMBER. Fall is coming, and I can't wait! This is my favorite time of year. The temperature is cooler, the sunshine is bright, and the air is fresh and clear. I love taking long walks around the trails near my home. This one is a particular favorite, and just when I start to really enjoy it—wham! A dirty birdy decides to leave his mark on my head.

How rude!

It's not the bird's fault. I guess he mistook my blue hat for the lake water I stood near at the time. It was both annoying and amusing. But it got me thinking about rudeness. How we as humans have gotten used to not being so nice. I've noticed an uptick in this behavior, so I thought I'd share.

What's the point of being rude?

What does it accomplish other than to make one feel good for half a minute after insulting someone else? I say half a minute because I think that's all it takes before "normal" humans begin to think about what they've just done or said and then start to feel guilty for behaving badly.

Rudeness is mean, unnecessary, and pointless. If unintentional, it's poor form at best. You can be blunt, frank, evasive, curt, short, assertive, insistent, and other words that escape me at the moment to get your message across overtly without hurting someone's feelings. To do that is at least honest. But blatant rudeness borders snarky with a middle finger up the "you know where" and, at best, passive-aggressive.

The Bible tells us that the tongue can be a mighty weapon. It warns against using it as such. We must watch what we say to avoid offense, and most people do. But, nowadays, being rude seems to be de rigueur and is far from decent, respectful, or nice.

Don't get me wrong. As humans, we will have our bad days now and again.

But it seems easier today to say something and run from the situation after. I heard someone call it drive-by insults of the hit-and-run variety. Some insults are hard to recover from. Rudeness is incredibly pervasive in our politics and online internet culture. Online, we can hide anonymously from our intended victim(s) without being found out. With our fingers on a keyboard, we can purge all our inner jealousy, resentment, and just plain meanness by posting something that would tear the guts out of our unfortunate victim without so much as batting an eye.

A second twinge of consciousness at doing so doesn't arise for some time afterward—but it does, eventually. On the flip side, the victim finds himself at a loss and tries to apologize and/or justify the reason for being insulted. Which, by and large, I think is a waste of time, but who asked me? Hide behind insults all you want, but rude is just…rude. It spills over into our everyday lives, leaving us scratching our heads in wonderment over what has happened to civility.

What has modern technology wrought?

I've run into rudeness more and more lately and find it repulsive and irritating. Clever words, or witty comebacks, to put the rude person in their place doesn't always come to mind, especially when it's unexpected. I either answer as if they haven't said anything disrespectful or just look at them without saying a word—then feel stupid afterward.

But why should I?

More to the point, why should I give them the satisfaction of any response or the idea that they've made me feel bad? Do I defend myself and attack, or just let the event pass? Should I laugh, shrug it off, or confront the offender? Confrontation could lead to escalation, and no one wants more of that. We have enough in our culture already. We ran out of "chill pills" a long time ago, and frankly, I think we need to bring those suckers back.

Does anyone else have this problem? Just asking.

More importantly, the problem is not mine but *theirs*. Of course it is! In the broad scheme of things, I don't want to think about what their "problem" might be. After all, rudeness doesn't deserve any more of my time *or* consideration than I care to give it.

However, I do wonder, like the dirty birdy, where we go from here. He just flew off without a care in the world. But as humans, we have feelings to contend with. Maybe we need to consider the source. Not to compare humans to birds, but that animal didn't give a sh*t (literally) about my feelings, and maybe neither should we when it comes to rudeness.

If you can't laugh at it, I think a dead stare in the face of the offender or simple silence is the best comeback of all.

Yeah!

Things to Do with Your Thumb

COMMON USAGE:

Hitchhike

Suck on it to pacify yourself as an infant.

Slide it into belt loops or hip pockets to look cool.

Help the other four fingers grasp/hold things, such as your special someone(s); any animal or object will do here.

Lick it when something tasty has been left behind on it, such as barbecue sauce or fried chicken…you get the idea.

Hold a "thumbprint" as unique to you as the size and shape of your ears.

A place to put a thimble.

Give approval/disapproval by giving the thumbs up or thumbs down gesture.

Give a sign of "I'm okay" by holding the thumb up.

INVENTIVE USAGE:

Eyeball measuring such as distance, picture framing, size of objects, etcetera.

Wind direction checks.

Point with it, a la Henry VIII or Elizabeth I, as some Hollywood celebrities are known to do.

Used when giving directions, such as where the "Thumb" is located in Michigan.

Point to yourself to express an emphatic, '**I**.'

OBSCURE:

Proudly show it to your neighbors, friends, and family as "green" when your garden looks exceptionally beautiful or successful.

Used to show as the number one or five when counting on your hands in certain countries.

Used as the door when playing the "church/steeple" hand game with children.

HELPFUL USAGE:

Help hold smelly things with your index finger until you get to the trash bin.

Help lift the tops of your eyelids.

Helps your toddler lift the top of your eyelids when asleep.

Help pinch the tush of your favorite loved one (amor, amour, amore).

Help snap a snappy rhythm or tune.

Help form the "O" in the "Okay" sign with the index finger.

Help pull up pants or other clothing items onto your body.

Help indicate "call me" with the help of your index finger.

Help silently indicate someone else is on the phone with the help of the index finger.

THINGS NOT TO DO WITH YOUR THUMB:
Slam it in a door.
Jam it where it doesn't belong, even if it fits. Suck on it as an adult.
Put it in harm's way.
Use it in conjunction with obscene gestures that can get you maimed or worse, such as tucking one in each nostril and then waving the other eight fingers at someone.
Flick buggers with it.
Balance a plate or cup on it.
And other ghastly things I can't come up with right now.

All I know is you should never use it to turn on an outdoor spigot with a Black Widow spider on it to water your lawn—as I DID!

Ergo, this list.

God

doesn't ask any more of

His angels

when

He knows they've

done their very

best.

The World is
imperfect.

That doesn't mean
we should be
imperfect in it.

Be your best
self.

L

O

N

E

L

Y

Either way you look at it,

there are many steps.

Be true to
who you are.

Love your
imperfections
because
they are the best
part of you.

Looking In from Outside

$$\frac{\text{WATER}}{\text{ME}}$$

(ME UNDER WATER Drowning)

DROWING.

$$\frac{\text{DIRT}}{\text{ME}}$$

(DIRT OVER ME. Suffocating)

SUFFOCATING.

ME

F ^{R} $_e$ E

(ME BREAKING FREE. Breathing)

BREATHING.

159

ABOUT THE AUTHOR

Donna Lawrence writes in the genre of women's fiction set in historical periods, even touching on coming-of-age in small-town America. *Miss Virginia and the Sweet Sisters* is her debut novel. Her second novel, *Pen Pals: A Novella and Other Stories*, is a novella with a compilation of short stories.

She is currently working on her third novel.

Looking In from Outside: Poetry & Prose is her debut poetry collection. Two of her poems, "The Rain" and "The Heir," are featured on the 9/11 Memorial Museum website.

Donna Lawrence was born and raised in Kentucky but has been a longtime resident of Colorado. Both states hold special meaning, and the many experiences she's had are ones she draws on in her writing. She also posts monthly on her blog, which provides a creative outlet when not working on her latest manuscript under Colorado's brilliant blue skies.

CONTACT

Crescent Hill Press
P.O. Box 200754
Denver, Colorado 80220

Email: donna@donnamarielawrenc.com
Website: www.donnamarielawrence.com